I'M A DINOMANIAC!

The Children's Museum

June 13 - Sept. 9

Eiteljorg

Museum

T5-AQQ-382

INDIANS of the EASTERN WOODLANDS

Troll Associates

INDIANS
of the
EASTERN
WOODLANDS

by Rae Bains

Illustrated by Mark Hannon

Troll Associates

Eastern Woodlands

Library of Congress Cataloging in Publication Data

Bains, Rae.
    Indians of the eastern woodlands.

    Summary: Describes the history, customs, religion,
government, homes, and people of the four main Indian
groups that lived in the woodlands of the Northeast.
    1. Woodland Indians—Juvenile literature. [1. Woodland
Indians. 2. Indians of North America] I. Hannon, Mark,
ill. II. Title.
E78.E2B34   1984   970.004 97   84-2664
ISBN 0-8167-0118-0 (lib. bdg.)
ISBN 0-8167-0119-9 (pbk.)

The first North American Indians encountered by the early explorers and settlers were the tribes of the Eastern Woodlands. They lived in the area extending south from Canada to the Gulf of Mexico, and west from the Atlantic Ocean to the Mississippi River. This large land area was covered by dense forests and had thousands of miles of streams, rivers, and lakes.

The Eastern Woodlands teemed with wildlife. The waters were filled with fish and shellfish. Corn, squash, and beans grew in the fertile soil. The Indians raised sweet potatoes and melons in the south, tapped maple sugar in the north, and harvested wild rice in the Great Lakes region. And wild berries and nuts could be picked off trees and shrubs everywhere. The land was rich with foods of all kinds.

Algonquin man

Iroquois woman

The Indians who lived on this land consisted of four main tribal groups. The first group was made up of many tribes of Algonquin Indians. They lived in the northeast, as did the second main group, the Indians of the Iroquois Nation. There were five separate tribes of Iroquois Indians in all.

9

Muskhogee

Seminole

Shawnee

Fox

Winnebago

Sauk

The third main group—the Creek Confederacy—lived in the southeast and consisted of a number of tribes. Among them were the Muskhogee and the Seminoles. The fourth group, which lived around the Great Lakes, was made up of several tribes, including the Sauk, Fox, Shawnee, and Winnebago.

The Algonquin Indians did some farming, but they were mainly hunters. They lived in small tribal villages scattered throughout the forests. Each tribe relied on the wildlife around its village. And when the game seemed to be thinning out, a tribe simply packed up and moved to a new location. Once they found fresh game, they set up a new village.

Every six months or so the Algonquin tribes came together for a powwow, or general meeting. Each village or tribe was represented by a chief at powwow councils. The powwow was an occasion for feasting and dancing, for settling arguments between groups, for forming alliances, and for trade.

Although each tribe was independent, the powwow gave a feeling of unity to the Algonquins. Together, the Algonquin tribes made up the largest tribal group in North America.

The Eastern Woodlands provided the Algonquins with materials for their tools, canoes, cooking implements, weapons, and homes. Algonquins had two kinds of homes —both called wigwams.

In their villages, the Algonquins lived in dome-shaped wigwams made of saplings covered by sheets of bark from birch, chestnut, oak, or elm trees.

When they were away from their village on a hunt, the Algonquins put up cone-shaped wigwams made of wooden poles and bark. These looked very much like the teepees of the Plains Indians.

There was a third kind of wigwam, called a wigwassawigamig, shaped like a book standing on its open edge with the spine on top. The wigwassawigamig was very large. Unlike the other wigwams, it could house more than one family and was sometimes used as a meeting room.

Although the Algonquins were primarily hunters, they were also excellent farmers. The Wampanoag Indians, who showed the Pilgrims how to fertilize corn fields with fish, were Algonquin. They taught the settlers to use corn in many ways and how to tap maple trees for the sap from which to make sugar.

The Algonquins also introduced the settlers to the clambake, at which clams, oysters, lobsters, mussels, and other shellfish were wrapped in seaweed and cooked in a pit dug in the earth.

The Indians of the Iroquois Nation, who came from five different tribes, called themselves the "People of the Long House." A long house was home for an extended family. An extended family included children, parents, grandparents, uncles, aunts, and cousins.

The women of the family owned the long house. When a brave married, he moved into the long house of his wife's family. The long houses were made of wooden-pole frames covered with bark, and they looked like long, large tunnels with round roofs.

The Iroquois Indians hunted deer and other woodland game, but farming determined the way they lived. An Iroquois tribe stayed in the same village for a number of years. Only when the large fields they farmed no longer produced a good crop of beans, corn, and squash did the tribe move to another location nearby.

The five tribes of the Iroquois Nation were united in a league. League meetings were held once a year and were attended by representatives from the Seneca, Cayuga, Onondaga, Oneida, and Mohawk tribes. The representatives discussed problems between themselves or between an Iroquoian tribe and a non-Iroquoian tribe.

The league could declare war against an outside enemy, if all the representatives agreed. But the league couldn't actually order anyone to fight. It was then up to each brave to fight or not. However, because fighting was an important part of Iroquois life, braves seldom turned down any opportunity to go into battle with an enemy.

The Iroquois' chief weapons included a wooden club with a pointed deer horn fixed to the end and a stone-bladed knife. Scalping, taking prisoners for use as slaves, and torturing prisoners were normal practices among Iroquois warriors. Of all the Eastern Woodlands Indians, the Iroquois were the fiercest.

Life for the Indians of the southeast was different from that of the northern tribes. The southeastern Indians of the Creek Confederacy lived in permanent villages and were primarily farmers and traders. Their homes, suitable to the warm climate, were usually wooden platforms raised off the ground.

The house of a southeastern Indian had a thatched roof and either fully open sides or walls around part of the house. A family often had a few houses, set around an open courtyard area. One house, with walls all around, was the permanent kitchen and a

sleeping place in cold weather. Another house, with a partial wall, was used as a living room and a warm-weather sleeping place. There was often a third house, for storing tools, food, and anything else a family owned.

The Indians of the southeast were accomplished farmers who raised corn, squash, sweet potatoes, and melons in their large fields. Each family had its own plot of land, but all the men and women of the village helped each other plant, cultivate, and harvest the crops. Everyone was expected to do a fair share of the work, and any person who shirked this responsibility had to pay a fine to the tribe.

When they weren't working, the southeastern Indians enjoyed festivals, games,
and sports. One of their favorite sports was
lacrosse. A lacrosse game was played on a
field five times as large as today's football
field.

Each team had about sixty players. One
team wore red body paint and represented
the red clan. The opposing team wore white
body paint and represented the white clan.

Each player carried two sticks. Each stick had a small thong basket at one end. No player was allowed to touch the leather lacrosse ball except with the stick or basket. The object was to score points by scooping up the ball in the basket and sending it through a pair of goal posts. The first team to score twenty goals was the winner.

The Woodlands tribes of the Great Lakes area had games that could be played in snow. One of these was called "snowsnake." A snowsnake was a long, smooth stick of maple wood, with one end carved to look like a snake's head.

To play snowsnake, the Indians packed down the snow on a long, level strip of ground. When the snow was packed hard and slick, the game began. Each player slid the stick along the ground, taking turns. The one who slid it the farthest was the winner.

Lacrosse sticks

Snowsnakes

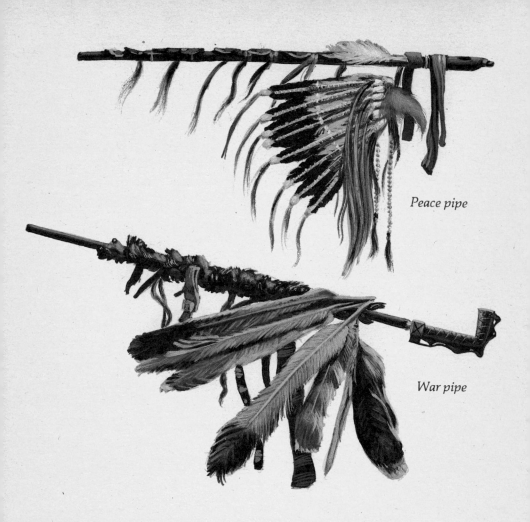

Peace pipe

War pipe

The Indians who lived around the Great
Lakes are sometimes called the "People of
the Calumet." The calumet, or peace pipe,
was a symbol of agreement and good faith.
Any Indian carrying a calumet was treated
with respect. Even during wartime the
calumet insured safe passage through
enemy territory.

The Great Lakes tribes had another ceremonial pipe. It was the war pipe. It was trimmed in red feathers, which stood for blood. The war pipe was passed around and smoked only when one tribe was declaring war on another tribe.

The Great Lakes Indians were excellent hunters, farmers, and food gatherers. Their diet, in addition to wild birds, game, corn, beans, and squash, included wild rice.

Wild rice was the staple food of these tribes. A grain that grows in the marshlands around the Great Lakes, wild rice was harvested by Indians who moved through the water in canoes. They knocked off the grains with sticks so that the wild rice fell into the canoes.

Like the eastern Algonquins, the Great Lakes tribes lived in dome-shaped wigwams. But the Great Lakes wigwams were covered with animal hides as well as bark.

The Indians hunted moose, caribou, beaver, otter, and many other small animals that were plentiful in this region. The skins were also used for clothing, footwear, and storage pouches.

With the coming of the settlers, life changed completely for the Eastern Woodlands Indians. The tribes were exposed to new diseases, against which they had no natural immunity. Their lands were taken away, and they were driven farther and farther west.

Some tribes tried to ally themselves with the British or the French, hoping to save themselves from extinction. Others fought back in what was always a losing battle. Today, all that remains of the Eastern Woodlands Indians are a few scattered reservations, a collection of Indian artifacts in museums, and the tales told by their descendants. The dense Eastern Woodlands and the tribes that lived in them are gone forever.